STRIKE ANYWHERE

STRIKE ANYWHERE

Poems by Dean Young

Winner of the Colorado Prize
Selected by Charles Simic

Center for Literary Publishing/University Press of Colorado

©1995 by Dean Young
Second Edition, 1998

Manufactured in the United States of America

Library of Congress Cataloging-in-Publication Data

Young, Dean,
        Strike anywhere: poems / by Dean Young.
        ISBN 0-870-81-423-0

Acknowledgments

Versions of some of these poems appeared in the following
magazines: *Colorado Review, Crazyhorse, Gettysburg Review, Indiana
Review, Organica, Ploughshares, Poetry East, Poetry Northwest, New
American Writing, Sulfur,* and *The Three Penny Review.* Thanks to
those editors.

"Upon Hearing of My Friend's Marriage Breaking Up" was
included in *Best American Poetry 1994.*

"Poem in Which Everyone Survives" was included in *Cape
Discovery: The Provincetown Fine Arts Work Center Anthology.*

Thanks to these friends for their responses to these poems:
David Rivard, Mark Halliday, Keith Ratzlaff, Clint McCown, Jim
Harms, Roger Mitchell, Dorian Gossy, Linda Charnes, Mary
Ruefle, David Wojahn, and Kevin Stein.

"All Told" and "Against Classicism" are for Lynda Hull.

Thanks to Loyola University of Chicago for leave time, which
was instrumental to the completion of the work, and the Illinois
Arts Council for an Individual Artist Gran. Special thanks to
Christina and Karen at University Press Books, Berkeley.

Jacket photo taken by Cornelia Nixon.

for Tony Hoagland
Cornelia Nixon
& in memory of Gloria Rhoads

A serious moment for the match is when it bursts into flame
And is all alone, living in that instant, that beautiful second for which it
      was made.

                                                Kenneth Koch

Contents

Upon Hearing of My Friend's Marriage Breaking Up, I Envision Attack From Outer Space

Even in September noon, the ground hog
casts his divining shadow: summer will never
end and when it does it will never come again.
I've only the shadows of doubts, shadows
of a notion. The leaves turn in tarnished
rain like milk. Hearts, rotund with longing,
explode like dead horses left in a creek,
our intentions misunderstood, misrepresented
like that day they turned the candles
upside down, thumped them out and we all
lost our jobs. Nothing personal. Handshakes around.
Of course we're not guilty
of what we've been accused of
but we're guilty of so much else, what's it matter,
I heard on the radio. I hate the radio,
how it pretends to be your friend.
You could be eating, you could be driving around
and then you're screaming, What, what did that fucker say
but by then it's someone else with the voice
of air conditioning saying, Take cover,
storm on the way. It's amazing
word hasn't gotten back to us from irritated
outer space how some creatures of spine and light
have finally had enough. Shut up, they beep back
but we're so dense, so unevolved, we think
it's just the usual interference: Bill next door
blending his Singapore Slings during Wheel
of Fortune. Right now they're working on something
that'll make our fillings fall out,
turn our checking accounts to dust,
something far more definitive.
There's a man starting his mower in the bedroom.
There's a woman burning photos in a sink.

2

I hate the phone, how it pretends to be
your friend, but I called you anyway,
got some curt, inchoate message that means
everyone's miserable, little shreds of your heart
rain down on me, twitching like slivered worms.
Upstairs, they're overflowing the tub again,
they're doing that Euripidian dance. I knew
a guy in college who stuck his head through a wall.
It seemed to decide something, to make us all
feel grateful, restored to simple things:
cars starting, cottage cheese, Larry, Curly, Mo.
It was, of course, a thin wall, a practice wall,
a wall between nowhere and nowhere's bedroom,
nothing like that 16th century woodcut
where the guy pokes through the sky into
the watchback of the cosmos. Tick, tick.
The cosmos gives me the creeps.
I like a decent chair where you can sit
and order a beer, be smiled at while you wait
for a friend who just had his sutures removed,
who rolls a quarter across his knuckles
to get them working again.

Ready-Made Bouquet

It's supposed to be Spring but the sky
might as well be a huge rock floating
in the sky. I'm the guy who always forgets

to turn his oven off pre-heat but I might
as well be the one with the apple in front
of his face or the one with Botticelli's
Flora hovering at his back, scattering

her unlikely flowers. Which is worse?
to have your vision forever blocked or
forever to miss what everyone else can
see, the stunning Kick me sign hanging
from your back? Is there anything more

ridiculous than choosing between despairs?
Part of me is still standing in the falling

snow with my burning chicken. In a black slip,
a woman despairs in front of her closet
five minutes before the guests arrive.
In the tub, a man sobs, trying to re-read
a letter that's turning into mush. Despair

of rotten fruit, of bruised fruit. The despair
of having a bad cat, garbage strewn over
your shoes, sofa in shreds. Despair of saying,
You bet I hate to part with him but I'm
joining the Peace Corps, to the girl who
calls about the ad. The despair of realizing

despair may be a necessary pre-condition

of joy which complicates your every thought
just as someone screaming in the hall, Get

4

away from me, complicates the lecture on
Wallace Stevens. Ghostlier demarcations,
keener sounds. Wallace Stevens causes despair

for anyone trying to write a poem or a book
called *Wallace Stevens and the Interpersonal.*
Sometimes interpersonal despair may lead to
a lengthy critical project's completion but how

could Jessica leave me in 1973 after pledging
those things in bed, after the afternoon looking
at Magrittes? The tuba on fire. The bottle with
breasts. Didn't I wander the streets half the night,

hanging out at the wharf, afraid of getting beat up
just to forget that one kiss in front of the bio-
morphic shape with the sign saying Sky in French.
The stone table and stone loaf of bread. The room

filled with a rose. Loving someone who does not
love you may lead to writing impenetrable poems
and/or staying awake until dawn, drawn to airy,
azure rituals of space ships and birds.
Some despairs may be relieved by other despairs

as in not knowing how to pay for psychoanalysis,
as in wrecking your car, as in this poem. Please
pass me another quart of kerosene. A cygnet
is a baby swan. Hatrack, cheese cake, mold.
The despair of wading through a river at night

towards a cruel lover is powerfully evoked
in Chekhov's story "Agafya." The heart seems
designed for despair especially if you study
embryology while being in love with your lab
partner who lets you kiss her under the charts
of organelles but doesn't respond yet

later you think she didn't not respond either
which fills you with idiotic hope very like
despair just as a cloud can be very like
a cannon, the way it starts out as a simple
tube then ties itself into a knot. The heart,
I mean. It seems, for Magritte, many things

that are not cannons may be called cannons
to great effect. David's despair is ongoing
and a lot like his father's, currently treated
with drugs that may cause disorientation and

hair loss. Men in white coats run from
the burning asylum. No, wait, it's not burning,
it's not an asylum, it's a parking lot
in sunset and they want you to pay. Sometimes
Rick thinks Nancy joined the Peace Corps just

to get away from him so later he joins the Peace Corps
to get away from someone else, himself it turns out,
and wades into a river where tiny, spiny fish
dart up your penis if you piss while in the river.
Don't piss while in the river is a native saying

he thinks at first is symbolic. The despair
of loving may lead to long plane rides with
little leg room, may lead to a penis full
of fish, a burning chicken, a room filled

with a single pink rose. Funny how
we think of it as a giant rose instead
of a tiny room.

While You Were at the Doctor's

I don't know what scares me more:
Tony's dream of sculpting the giant head
or the blood on the pillow case.
Or the three OKs spray painted in the street:
yellow, blue, black
like the backward progress of a bruise.
And the mark on the window where a bird crashed.
How it looks like a kiss with feathers stuck to it.
That's what I am: a man looking through a crash print
thinking it a kiss.
And the little brown bird shaking its head.
And how after you die I'll probably eat chocolate again.
And shrimp.
Carefully pulling off the tiny legs,
piling them on the side of my plate.
I'll hear the ocean again, tugging.
Licking its lips.
I'll lie in a hammock again.
I'll hear rowboats knock against the pier
even when there are no rowboats near.
No rowboats no rowboats no rowboats near.
I think again this year I didn't get the bulbs deep enough.
Mostly my friends left town
then so did I. I tried to look on it
as an opportunity like the start
of Daylight Savings Time.
And how in his dream the giant head starts talking.
For this pain, for that pain murmur the syrups
on the bathroom shelf as if that's what any of us want.
How my aunt finally just put gravel in a cake.
How the snow tussles against the trees
like Death in Emily Dickinson.
Wolves eat mostly mice all winter.

Something long and gleaming, cold and steel introduced.
I love how the wind snatches away the cloud's mask
as if that's what any of us want.
How actuality splits open like an orange
within a symbolic universe of filthy, churning waters.
Sticky sweet, full of seeds.
Last night I dreamt again of thrashing
and you on the far shore.
By what manner is the soul joined to the body?
How my parents offered no warning
that day I stuck my fork into the socket.
The worst part was liking it, the burst bulb of my head.
You'll be fine, the costly, frosty voice
intoned above me. Sure, I thought,
Can you bring back my dog? What do you know
about broken violins? All those years of tension
then they just split apart.

Acupuncture

Rain on the ridge of burned stumps,
a face carved from one emerging
of course screaming and what doesn't
emerge screaming? You dream you're
being devoured by ants. Lashed and
in flames, you wait in a waiting room
lit with flowers but artificial flowers,
artificial light. Perhaps all matter
is just screaming congealed. Perhaps
God loves pain, his only form of exercise.
Mostly the body just lies there, not
making a sound like a book left open
in the rain, a piano with the lid down.
I believe the body is a book left open
in the rain just as I believe the body
is a piano often out of tune. It's the
tuning that defeats me. The reading.
Feeling the breaks in her lips while
kissing. It's the beauty that defeats me.
One face looking east smiling, one west
downcast. The practiced contortions
of musicians bringing forth such grace.
Small flowers by the roadside
growing straight from rock.

Pacific Decorum

I know it would be best if I didn't
say anything about God. Yet I am put
in front of an ocean where even
a pile of stones defeats me. I should
warn you of my emotion. Ignore it.
I will need a moment only of swallowing.
A minor devotion. I think if I could lift
a single stone, under it would be
a light like none I've ever seen.
Thick like glue. I know this is ridiculous.
Perhaps if I said please. Please waves.
Please music. The radio announcer seems
practiced at murmuring underwater. Somehow,
enough agreement for a symphony although
the violins say, Up here; the trumpets,
Fire! Fire! Perhaps we should go and
be killed by the last elephants, trampled,
gored although I am afraid we might not
deserve it. I think this heart must be
discarded so the next one will grow.
With redder bark, lower berries, sturdier
thorns. Yes, go ahead, smoke. During
last night's hilarity, my lamp fell over,
breaking its concentration. See, I'm
all right. I've made a joke this early
in the day. Still, I keep thinking about
God, about how the body's always torn
apart, and lost. No, sorry. Allow me
instead to tell you of my friend's wife
bending his fingers for a month, flexing
his legs, yammering about their pregnant
daughter in Wyoming who had stayed
by the hospital bed as long as she could.
Even the internist said, finally,

it took a miracle although the story's
always told differently. As if brought
to court. But it's the version with
the castle, the lion composed of fire
that gets me. From an otherwise sensible
man. Told with reluctance. Nothing
about his car tumbling from the bridge.
Please don't start the opera now. No,
I don't want something warm to drink.
I've read that it's just the random
last discharging of nerves: the lion,
the castle, like water dribbling from
a turned-off hose. Nerves. Someone
always burning. Imagine bundles of thread
with fevers. The ant's singing to herself.
Wounded and spinning. Stuck in the nectar
and singing. Imagine climbing a mountain
with thirty pounds of wet rope on your back
only it's not rope, it's electricity,
it's not a mountain, it's your father's
face. This is the segment of the program
where they ask for a pledge. See how calm
I can be, sitting and listening to KPFA,
watching the water where a ship has appeared.

Poem in Which Everyone Survives

Luckily what I thought was a storm turns out
to be the giant head of Frank O'Hara roiling up
to thank me for bringing him to Bloomington in 1973.
Seven years dead, he hadn't even started to stink,
the bugs hadn't even gotten to him with their
systematic readings. He only smelled of hot asphalt,
ball bearings, mustard, flowers of course but
flowers that eat meat. He smelled like a body
all right but one asleep. What's that you got there,
my friends asked, another immense dead moth? I mean
in the middle of nowhere, my shoulders not even
aching and everyone trying to sing along and
the trees in their 20th, 30th, 40th youths,
smearing their lips on the ground, their dicks
in their hands. So like a fool, I asked, Where
are we going, even with my expensive tutelage
in not asking, my erudition in not listening.
We goeth unto Death, spake Frank and what did I
expect? Death with his vintage wardrobe, his
yard full of used stoves, hubcaps, his way of mis-
accenting syllables so what we've been hearing
all our lives sounds suddenly awful, pained like
a song can be pained almost forever by someone
weeping through it, like a movie that loses
everything good about the book, its fierce
interiority like the eye of the paramour, how
he's pecked the neck of his intended so she's
nearly decapitated, ferruginous, blinking
out of both sides of her head like being loved
by Picasso, always from the first time. Is lost.
Insert "is lost" back there somewhere. I love
how sentences, like lives, can follow their own
glittering vein into the mountainside like
that moment when the keys are tossed between

us, suspended, and the moment after when one of us
is gone until Steve, who I haven't seen in years,
suddenly calls, who I suddenly got to New Orleans with
the day after Mardi Gras, 1975, masks blowing
down the street like fragments of Sappho, my wrist
in a cast, driving all night, whose girlfriend I
didn't sleep with even after they broke up and
she came up behind me and kissed my ear while
I watched a wasp crashing against the window, drunk,
and aren't we all crashing against the invisible
but do we want in or out? Whack. Whack. And this
the shorter version. He's back from New Zealand
after forgetting about her the way I jumped out
of an airplane to forget someone else, picking
kiwis as a kind of penance for falling in love
the way parachutes are penance for gravity,
libraries for authors, sneezing for breath,
life for death and sometimes he'd just squeeze
one out of its hairy tuft right into his mouth
under the New Zealand sun which he says is
yellower than ours just as the kiwi bushes
were full of tame yellow birds about their
yellow business of living forever just as
the night must be about its business of
darkness. I mean in the middle of nowhere and
none of us had bled to death internally exactly yet.

Centrifuge

It might have been midnight when last we talked
and now I've got this poem that keeps flying
apart which accounts under these xenophobic stars
for all force: gravity, magnetism, wind, the ling-

ering of a kiss, a judo throw although
there's yet to be a single formula for it.
Save us from single formulas. One room
smells like ash, another smells like fruitcake.

One cardinal sits on a branch, another under.
You've got to be a bird to understand any of this,
feathery and hollow-boned. You've got to be
a claims adjuster staring at a storm. You've

got to be entered by a shower of gold coins.
On the back of the Brazilian book of poems,
the translator looks haggard as if she's chased
a mule cart into another century, the twentieth,

and suddenly she's feeble in Pittsburg in her
bunny furs. Imagine suddenly Pittsburg,
the handful of dust thrown up for the sun's
haughty inspection, laughing its molecular

laugh, hungry again, dazzling again in its
stained satin pajamas like the memory of lost
love. I think we were walking through some woods
towards more to drink, up ahead the future

gesticulating wildly like a beggar who'd
scare us out of money, the future threatening
to isolate us like glum geniuses prowling
record stores, not getting a lot done,

mistaken for clerks with gum on our shoes. I'm
trying not to panic. I'm trying to find the center,
drive a nail through it like a mercy killing. I'm
letting myself be thrown around while Come at me

says the day to the night, Come at me says
the cloud to the moon dragging its terrible noose.
Come at me says L so she can show me what she's learned
in martial arts and now some part of me can't or

won't get up, the ground husky with thaw, fall's
idiot nomenclature garbled in the bramble. I'm
letting my back get soaked. I'm turning into
wine. I'm a broken kore, lips barely parted saying

what? I know suffering does not make us beautiful,
it makes us disappear like wearing black shirts
at midnight, like lying on the spinning earth
crying, Momma, Momma.

The Decoration Committee

A poem telling the story of a man shooting a moose
is a narrative poem.
If the poem goes on for a long time and the moose
turns out to be his daughter who got screwed
by the lecherous, jealous gods and the man
then founds a city, it is an epic.
Many say the Age of Epic is behind us,
the rain falls upon the moose corpse
and the murderous, capricious gods seem done with us,
killed or wandered off, and, unattended,
unhouselled, we charge through the bracken
with only the burning hoof print of human love
upon us. Perhaps the long poem you struggle with
is just a long poem as a big storm
need not be a hurricane. When I was a child,
hurricanes, like battleships, were given
exclusively women's names. Advances
have been made and currently hurricane Bill
is rampaging through Jamaica, an island already
wracked with poor prenatal care. There is still
so much to do. Each is alone, shorn and bleeding
of lip, mouth crammed with feathers, hands full
of torn lace, the curtain rising on all
the people who murdered and loved each other
now bowing arm in arm. A conductor appears,
balding, and the crowd disperses to cafes
to argue and woo. How to know what next
to do, where move, what does and doesn't
belong here in a place we've been a hundred times
but never noticed the pictures of burning
buildings on the walls. Oh, what was once
a forest is no longer a forest, what was once
a tree is now a wheel. A poem, usually shortish,
which begins, "When I was a child" or

goes on about clouds or trees or lost love:
woe, woe, etc. is a lyric poem. The original
lyre was made from a hollowed-out tortoise shell.
From the tortoise's point of view,
the lyric was a complete catastrophe
but it has done very well by humans although
I know of no studies concerning if and in how many cases
a lyric poem eases heartache by initiating 1.
the beloved's return, the door flies open,
the bra unstrapped, the moose dappled
with dew and/or 2. a getting-over-it
happiness at just having written/read the poem
which is about misery in the old way
but also in a new way and then noticing
the pretty barmaid. How little
we know of Sappho beyond the eloquent
snips of limb-loosening Eros. Chervil,
a spice, is mentioned for its tenderness.
Other examples abound.
Robert Frost's "Stopping by Woods
on a Snowy Evening" is thought by some
to be about Santa Claus, by others
suicide. Generally, the sucide people
have higher degrees. Anguish seems endless.
The heart however is often frivolous
perhaps as a form of defense
akin to the gaudy coloration of the tender
poison arrow frog. I am beautiful therefore
invulnerable is the message of its body.
In English, there appears to be no rhyme
for "orange." Many poems fill many books
and in this they resemble the records
of small claims courts. One of the ways
new kinds of poems may be written
is by finding out what people agree is not poetry
and doing that. Where are the timorous mortals
banged by gods? Whare are the trees and woe?
Ben Johnson, referring to a disease of sheep,

said that some subjects cannot be made poetic
but then along came the French.
After hours of voodoo drumming, everything
you do may seem like a poem.
Poems cannot be "fixed."
If at the end only a few people are dead
and the rest mill about the fountains
as if waiting for a wedding, it is a comedy.
Who are the bride and groom? Maybe me,
maybe you. Who cares? Let the doors
burst open upon worlds of light, dogs chasing
brooms, the moose out there somewhere braying
for its mate. Is it not nearly enough to sway
to the invisible music, to watch the wrinkley
waters? To feel within the heart the crushed ball
of aluminum foil?

Beside the Bodies of the Broken-Hearted

The day after is entirely different than
the day before just as an astronaut is
different after blast-off. He may become
devout, he may crave horribly a gin fizz.
Sharp implements must be taken away. Not
a cheery day, the swans in rut stand and
strut across the water like menacing hats.
The leaves churn and spin like the heart
of my friend who once again has lost
the girl he loves. Monday he didn't know,
quaffing at the bar. Today he knows.
Word comes from downstate she wants her
couch. It is difficult moving a couch
down some stairs with a person who has
lost the girl he loves. You cannot trust
him at the top and you cannot trust him
at the bottom. Suddenly he wants to drive
real fast to the jewelry store, he needs
to see a diamond scratch glass, he's talking
nonstop or nary a sound while the alcohols
affect him not. You do not want to find
yourself beside the body of the broken-
hearted when flowers are delivered. Or
not delivered. Or just ripped from the dirt.
You do not want to open the door
without first feeling if it's hot.

Errata

I turned the assemblage upside down,
positioned the gusset flush with the rabbet.
Folded the lower hanging end up and right,
forming what would be the front of the bow.
Did the full left turn past 8 to stop at

34. Used caution with contents under pressure.
Softened the butter. Inserted and adhered.
Called and culled. Meandered buggish upon
the clinquent plain. Misconceived, re-
convened. Arrived at the gates one hour

before departure. Splintered pencils.
Dead-headed cosmos. Flattened leaves
in a book identifying leaves. Held
the bucket. Memorized and forgot
amino acid configurations, French vocabulary,

directions from Chicago to Peoria, the generals
of *The Iliad* and where they came from.
Who survived. One wishes to avoid the sense
of being trapped inside a plastic garbage sack
although the sense of breaking out

may be cathartic. The tears so blue,
you palpate like an asteroid. You start things
and it's difficult to end them
like an affair that begins with the simple
desire to see a magnificent body naked

but then achieves the consistency of sap.
Alternately, you start things
and it's difficult to keep them going

like an affair that begins with the simple
desire to see a magnificent disrobing but

then deepens like the color of clothing
wet with rain. Rain after months of no rain
and the desert blooms. As if there was such a thing
as a simple desire. One is not likely
to forget or, for a while, be able

to drink even a glass of orange juice without
pain. One shops for new fish for the aquarium,
tries not to go only to the same places.
The novel progresses until *thunk*—parts
six seven eight. The horse trots over

to the gate, accepts your proffered
weeds. One tries not to be a ghost
even if that means wearing at sunset a red hat.
Being impossible with waitresses. Not signalling.

Still, one tries to go on making, following
instructions. It is best to assemble first
without glue as practice, then disassemble,
glue and reassemble but who has patience
for that? One fucks up and regrets but

sometimes not too terribly because they've
included extra screw blocks, extra screws.
Plethoras of putties. Everyone will understand
why you arrive so late, so barehanded.
The swans are back on the lake.

Spring Figure

In Punxatawny the ground hog sees his shadow.
Persephone has no shadow, only a herd of pigs.
In Graceland, the shadow of Elvis is unmistakeable.
In my wishful thinking, the murderer sees his shadow
and drops his gun, the president sees the 13
shadows of his cabinet and stops babbling.
Bottles throw their drunken shadows down from shelves,
the eyelashes of movie stars throw shadows
shaped like dollar signs across our laps.
A shadow falls over us then what throws the shadow
falls over us. The son cast out of the kingdom,
his equipage travels in shadow. Wallace Stevens
casts a big shadow. Abe Lincoln's shadow seems
bent and tarnished. Even words throw shadows
writes William Gass in an essay on Jasper Johns.
In a famous painting the 3 throws its 2-shaped
shadow although it may be the other way around.
The rabbit throws the shadow of a contorted hand.
Plato says all we ever see is shadows of the ideal.
Sometimes when I'm with you, I'm excited as if
we were under the shadow of a piano. In California
Bob sits in luxurious shadow that avocados
fall through. Some people object to everything.
What I thought was my death was only shadow
carried by crows. What I thought was dim writing
was only a shadow from the other side. Homer
says there are shadows underground. I need
more light are famous last words. Already
the end has thrown its shadow over the beginning.

Roving Reporter

I'm perfectly sure it's not about being saved
or living this life as preparation. It's about
waking in a strange bed, suitcase lost,
children smacking eels against the dock,
the impenetrable rotation of the guards,
adumbrations of cloud.

It's clutching the chair leg crying, Help
on a chunk of ore
whistling through the cosmos.

Last night,
under the glowing highrise,
I shouted Charlotte into the epileptic stars
until the revelers, already hating me,
brimmed with fear.

Yellow pinpricks opened in my head,
first contact with the big blackout.

Maybe I was trying to shout
Charlotte clear out of existence
the way insistence becomes erasure,
a repeated word a senseless blue beginning.

Maybe there never was a Charlotte I wanted so,
followed to this island that was once a leper colony
now full of guys in epaulettes holding open doors.

Maybe I'm just
a figment in someone's dream I never
really knew, a prop in someone else's symbolism
of repression and need. Aren't we just each other's
nocturnal inklings? Isn't the world a drunken sleep?

I mean I might have known a Charlotte once
whose letters seemed to come from quarantine,
parts of animals enclosed as proof of what
I did to her: feather, moth wing, cricket's leg
like a violin bow upon a rumpled bed.

I remember red
streamers tied to a fan's wire face.
I remember heat. Somewhere above me I know
the golden body sleeps, fussed over by giant bees,
the distillates of a thousand lilacs
drooling from their jaws.

My Work Among the Insects

The body of the lingerneedle is filled
with hemolymph unconstricted except
for a single dorsal vessel. A ventral
diaphragm bathes the organs of the head,

undulations drawing the fluid back through
tiny holes called ostia aided by the movement
of a Napoleon within each abdominal segment
pacing his Elba exile, muttering la Russie

la Russie as the snow squeaks beneath
his boots. All through the night
the temperature drops but no one
knows where the lingerneedle goes.

Yet it emerges each spring like
a baseball team. Gertrude Stein
may have been referring to this when
she wrote, A hurried heaving is a quartz

confinement, although what we normally think of
as referring is brought into question by her work.
A hive of white suching. At the time
of her death, she owned many valuable

paintings renowned for ugliness.
Gertrude Stein grew up in Oakland
but an Oakland as we know it not. No
plastic bags snagged in the trees. Semi-

automatics had yet to reach the fifth grade.
A person could stand in a field, naked
and singing. Sure, there was blood but
there were rags for wiping up the blood.

Deciduous trees, often confused by California
climes, just bloom whenthehellever like how
people have sex in French movies. Here,
during the cool evenings and hot mid-days,

the mild winters and resistive texts,
the lingerneedle thrives. Upon the ruddy
live oak leaves appears its first instar,
spit-like but changing shortly to a messy lace

erupting into many-legged, heavy-winged
adults that want only to mate. Often in July,
one finds them collapsed in the tub, unable
to gain purchase on the porcelain that seems

to attract them mightily. It is best not
to make everything a metaphor of one's own life
but many have pressed themselves against cool
and smooth, in love and doomed. Truly

the earth hurtles through the cosmos at
an alarming rate. Recent research suggests
a gummy discharge of the mating pair

has promise as an anti-coagulant. Please,
more money is needed. The sun sets. The air
turns chilly and full of jasmine.

While Tony Hoagland Reads at The Poetry Society of America

I am not worried much. The music is very
loud. Two inches of snow killed everything
outside but there is still some blooming
inside, the last of my cosmos drizzling
their yellow pollen uselessly upon my desk.
First I imagine him threading the dark
urbane crowd full of robbers and the robbed.
There is something different about his face,
a book held forward open, a few words I
can't read. Maybe French. Maybe German.
Evening stars haggle for position, leaves
on the ground dissolving, unfolding, losing
their hints of color, unsolvable. I'm trying
to boil something chthonic off the bottom
of my good pot. I rise periodically to check
the darkening water, particulates whirling
like a hypnotic sleep. I think he's wearing
that jacket with the silver lining ripped.
What did God mean, arming him so insufficiently,
sending him into the blue part of the flame?
Why is God opening flowers now, this late
in November, flowers in all the faces,
directional as compasses drawn by some mad
abberant magnetism. I think he's walked away
from wrecks worse than this, the car come
to rest in a ditch after ricochetting through
the on-coming but I think he's not entirely
safe at the Poetry Society of America
sandwiched between two shrink-wrapped poets
who sound rather English. It is impossible
to imagine them pissing outside on such a cold night.
At some point, the tables of higher society
had 19 pieces in a single place setting.
What are we to do with all these spoons,

the degrees of serration on the knives?
We are at a difficult moment for King Crimson
in the song called The Law of Maximum Distress
Part One but soon the tape will run out
and by the time it gets restarted, alliances
will have formed between the violin and
mellotron. There will be this mounting
then a whine and then a sense of how hard
it is for the univese to exist in time,
all that unaccountable weight we only think
is emptiness, how else this bent light,
these thousand centers and then a quiet
plucking, a sense of what a relief it is
to be the universe filled with open spaces,
everything racing from everything else
and then the stoned hippies at Zurich Volkshan,
November 15th, 1973, cheering and shouting for more.

Note Enclosed with My Old Jean Jacket

Herein lies what I lived through and with
and tore to fit over my cast, fell down in,
rose up in, wept and slept in on carpets
of peanut shells, on clouds and tombstones
and soggy chairs, on the bent weaponry of
remote women, my glimpse of the garden
occluded by dreams of hundred dollar bills.
It all goes up the nose fast but somehow
I survived, put on weight, took up some
unpredictable space like the woman from Iowa
abducted by a UFO who now has a few things
to say to the media. I too have been far away
and heard the extraterrestrial hum and feared
I'd be dissected. I too have heard the crickets
of earth straining their leash in thin weeds,
anxious, anxious for the record stores to open.
It seemed at any moment a new music was about to be
discovered like an inland passage to a golden
shrine and all would be familiar as the beloved's
name heard in a crowd, my jacket unwashed but
absolved, patched by a woman who joined
the Peace Corps and lost all her hair
to a disease that mostly afflicts chickens.
I seethed and yearned like the suicidal sea,
my jacket weighing over me no more than a couple
size D batteries, not nearly as much as all the meat
I've eaten amassed if one imagines such a frightening
karmic mess like all the time we spend asleep joined
end to end, horror of dark accumulation. Oh,
I'm nearly lost sending you this jacket. Always
something lost and ripping, thick tears spilling
through us, drying like my jacket draped
over the radiator after sleet. We
were young and toughing out a season

in our sneakers as we tried to kill the Buddha,
tried out madly for the fencing team, seething
and yearning in our jeans, first to be cut,
aimlessly driving while someone fussed
with the radio buttons. It was like a game,
divided into sides, everyone screaming
the same thing to entirely different
purposes. You'd get up, pull on pants, shirt,
jacket, then what? You'd finger the scar
ringing your skull from where they put
this brain in you. You remember being hoisted
into lightning. You remember something terrible
and unintentional by a stream and the villagers,
enraged, approaching the castle. Maybe it was all
a mistake, your few happy nights in the woodland,
your invitation to the wedding where the beautiful
stranger kisses you on the ear. For a while it seemed
like it could last forever as long as you did some
sewing yourself. People were necking in idling cars.
The snatch of song make out in passing seemed
rotund with longing just as the trees seemed
withered with longing and the man who promised
to throw money from his window was hustled away
in the night by those named in his will. They tried
to convince us it was all for our protection:
those flashing lights behind us, the fierce visors
girls in miniskirts were wearing, the seal
on medicine that seemed impossible to break
so for a while we hung on to all sorts of junk
we didn't need, couldn't wear, our size
had changed. It was a way of avoiding menace
we thought, a way of forestalling loss, pretending
it was something we'd already been through, suffered,
survived that the years had made quaint, inert,
the way we feel cozy looking at photos of people
long ago dead, the way we think what killed them
will never kill us yet we're just as helpless
pawing for the dropped key in the dark, equally

confused about what can bring us light, about what,
exactly, electricity is. We thought it was a day like
any other with a dental appointment at 2 and our dreams
rusting away like old baby carriages. It was simple,
just drive to the store for something new,
for something more. So what there was the usual
haggle over parking and someone in the noodle aisle
had to discipline his child and what was once
revolutionary song was converted to ether
in pipes over our heads? How secure the milk
in its firm prediction of spoilage and that too
somehow comforts us, convinces us to quit
for a moment our long treatise on death. We
could drink it after all, all of it, stand
right there with it gurgling out the sides
of our mouth but of course that sort of thing
isn't done. Why? Well, it was agreed upon
while you were out of the room like the rules
of poker, a game you'll never win or lose
much at. And our desires? Well, they went
running off ahead of us as usual towards
the lake with ducks, a-wag, tennis ball in mouth
and we felt some odd sense of well-being, coiling
the leash up in our hand, loping after. It turns out
so much in the world actually works and no one
right now wants to remind us of all those
messes we've left for someone else to mop up.
There's healing all around, scabs are forming
and flaking away and even the fat, legless lady
with her pekinese seems another shape of love
just beyond our comprehension. It turns out,
all that time, vast conspiracies of forgiveness
were mustering in the sky and we had only to look up
to receive. Starlight. The resemblances of clouds.
Of course these frightening moments persist,
we really are going to pieces but surely
we can't go on dragging all this stuff around with us,
no matter what it means, which may, even this,

nearly rag, permanently soiled, passed-on,
constitute a gift.

Vermeer

The largest group of Vermeers hangs
in Amsterdam. Many travel to Amsterdam
to look at Vermeers as well as De Hooches
and Ter Borches. There is also a dark district
where one may be included in unspeakable acts
well within the traveler's budget. First name
Jan pronounced nearly Yawn. Painter of luminous
quiet, rivaled only by Van Eyck in depiction
of spiritual reflection. Vermeer sold few
paintings in his lifetime. He had to wait
200 years to stop being a failure. Do not
get the hiccups while looking at Woman
Reading a Letter as you will be asked
to leave. Ditto sneezing, belching, coughing,
all of which disperse acids known to destroy
masterpieces. Due to the language barrier,
your removal may be accomplished with
rigorous gesture. Whatever Dutch is written
in the letter is obliterated by light.
Such is the fate of spiritual reflection.
How little I actually know about Vermeer
and how loath I am at the idea of finding out more.
Oddly, Vermeer was said to have had a large
penis although not as large as John Dillinger's.
Like many artists, he communicated in code.
His relation to the female figure is part
oblong to conic section, part man in tight
underwear. One leaves the Vermeers, unlike
the work of French masters, with an unsated
need for a glimpse of the naked babysitter.
In Vermeer, women appear both nunnish and
knocked-up. Some questions are best not asked.

Lives of Composers

Once I knew a girl named Dawn
who played the part of a swan
in a ballet. Who rejected me
when I became engorged with blood.
As far as I'm concerned, that's it
for ballet. I hid in a drawer.
Something's left out of that last
sentence but it's what everyone
hides in a drawer. At the hospital I was caught
racing wheelchairs and told to stop
acting like a child. At that moment
my childhood ended, some god grabbed
my hair and smashed my head like
a clavichord. The next time my childhood
ended it seemed like the 19th century
in spite of all the gadgets. Previously
my father had shown no propensity for
Romantic poetry aside from a hacking
cough. Now "the ghostly hand upon
the windowpane, remembered cataracts,
ministries of frost," that stuff.
From there on in I had to do
everything myself. Much rode upon
the rutabaga crop. My instrument
was held too tight, my instructor
hollered. You must cup a whisper,
touch only vanishing. I couldn't
believe he was getting paid for this.
There was nothing hopeful about
his medicine chest. In the book,
Lives of Composers a single story
materializes: long journey from
the old country then years and years

of yearning, the feeling of missing
something big taking up the shape
of a champagne cork in your throat.
You're running in shoes completely
unintended for running. You remember
a day you lay in a field of adder's tongue.
It was late, sunset or dawn, you'd be
in trouble when you got home but
you thought you could dance, thought
you heard a song.

Charm School

It's that brief time, no more than 3 days,
when you sit outside and tiny, unarmored green bugs
traipse all over you. Delicate, perplexed,
oblivious maybe, maybe amorous,
supplicant after a moment of clinging,
or ranting, working their vast jaw apparatus,
a little singing from the back legs before
they fall apart into the 16 or 17 molecules
of which they're made. Alms, alms.
I love how they get messed up in my arm hair,
how they signal and collapse. Who knows
what forest they wonder in. Who knows
where they're going or if they're just blown about
like seeds or broken kites or why they are so stupid
to go up your nose or in your ears;
not like fleas sipping at the corner of the eye,
not like yellowjackets scouting for meat,
their intentions are vague as prepositions.
Who knows what autumn they are already in. Oh,
can't we save them or just understand them which
reminds me of Kenneth Koch who I've always
wanted to meet, well, not exactly meet because
almost everyone I've wanted to meet then met
has turned out to be a disappointment, not him or her
exactly, more the meeting itself like concrete
that doesn't set, the pole just goes on wobbling.
No, I'd just like to say hello and thank him
for how his poems blurt out things like
Oh, can't we save them! although he read
at the college where I work the year before
I got there and the guy who picked him up
at the airport now hates him. Imagine,
hating Kenneth Koch. Imagine hating
peach trees. Maybe we expect to understand too much

or expect too much from understanding. Like how
we showed the nursery man a sprig of the bush
we wanted, swiped from down the street and how
one of his eyes looks slightly off as if something
worrisome was right behind you so he'd probably be
a good person to have with you in a dangerous
situation but would also, and maybe because of,
always make you nervous, but we weren't nervous,
we were excited even as he scratched his head
where the hair used to be, all nervousness
is excitement but all excitement isn't nervous,
and went inside and got the big book and found
Dipelta Yunnanensis to match our snip and
description of the papery bark and silhouette
but no, he never had any of those and it was
too late to get any this year but he'd put us
on a list. It seemed he had once had tragedy
in his life, had wrecked everything but somehow
found his way to opening a nursery and becoming
healed and deliberate and wise as only people
who've wrecked their lives can get. He filled
our small car with 6 lilacs instead.
4 purple dwarfs, 2 French hybrids. Imagine
doing nothing but that, lifting the young plants
by their wrists, loading cars with more than
anyone would think could fit. Imagine having
six green eyes. Imagine what an emerald sees.
Imagine our ride home, sky fat with storms
passing through, a white peony face down
in the dirt, heavy with opening and rain.
Imagine being that close to death.

Paradise

Behind the Art Building, the weather's
starting to have its hydrochloric way
with the rows of practice plaster Adam
and Eves but in the woods the bronze pair
have withstood everything but the radical
lesbians' ballpeen attack on Adam. Something
about the distance between them spells trouble,
something about the position of their hands,
the distance and position of all of us.
Sometimes you're left on the strained
edge of things, provoked, rebuked,
a part of you pounded on, the sky burning
with various declines, your heart burning,
your credit rating burning. Someone
should have warned you about how years later,
after you finally admitted what she
had always been waiting to hear, after
you just looked into the trees and read aloud
what you saw there, even those words
would come to mean something different
than you thought; how later, in the back
of the rehearsal hall, you'd watch your part
on stage, ballooned all out of proportion
as if from a pituitary imbalance, the scene
stopped and started further back with
everyone moved slightly left, the lights
less direct. It seemed to be someone taller
but more rat-faced who said what you said
with the emphasis totally skewed. It was
another lesson those statues seemed to offer,
how the variations are nearly endless even
of things that already happened. It's
a little like being under a fallen chandelier
then everyone rushing up, saying, Are you all right?

and you can't really tell because you're so embarrassed
to be asked. Hard to say if the hands are opening
or closing, beseeching or fisting up. It's like
how you felt having that talk with the folks
that was intended to make a few things clear
about who you were now that you were older,
through with their meddling, but days later
you'd find that cake tin shaped like a swan
and remember all that fluffy coconut frosting
and realize how undeserving you were, are, probably
always will be there on the floor in your kingdom
of leaks. Get up! You think you're the only person
in the world? The main problem is only
one of scale—your weeping soldier dwarfs
the station where he must wait for the toy train.
He's bigger than the trees. You'll need
to travel a different way. You'll need to beg
forgiveness but no more than anyone else.
Just left out on the strained edge of things,
it reminds you of a mouth. It reminds you
of something you dreamt and later
interpreted, were encouraged to interpret
not as expulsion, but as memory of birth.
No wonder the street splits open around us
like fruit with its red palpitations, like the sea
we travel through, glinting, not really intent
on getting anywhere, just avoiding everyone else
doing the same thing, avoiding the shallows
with their dull, insistent weeds and the bridge
embankments. Of course we were standing up there
too, on that bridge watching ourselves all the time,
not sure we were watching the right thing,
jittery that something was about to be revealed
as the trucks lumbered behind us like furious gods
bearing their perishable goods. You'd only get
one chance but there was that other time
while the daughters played croquet on the lawn,
their bridesmaids' dresses wet with dew, when

your friend confessed and started to cry and
you were afraid how little you felt, afraid
the capacity to feel had leaked from you
like oil from a cracked urn. Yet whatever you said
must have been enough as he gathered himself in,
tugged up those silver nets that bring forth
such collapsed monsters from the psychic deep.
He's thanking you, apologizing in a short note
he'll send with a clipping about a man
giving the teller a holdup note with his name
and address on the back. And don't we all
want to be caught? Want someone to shout,
Stop! Hands up! so at last we can relax
under their cool vigilance, tell all to our captors
who sooner or later start blabbing too
about how they ended up with this lousy job
when really they just wanted to open a cafe,
saying their children's first names, how their fathers died.

Immortality

I'm hating myself for the last time
I saw you, let you buy your own shots—
my ex-girlfriend's best friend whose
ex-boyfriend I gave a hundred for
the abortion years ago. I remember
the dark interior of your oceanic Plymouth
ripped and frothing. I remember slurring
my hands over you as you drove and pushed
me off, laughing. I saw the solution
to our loneliness like two puzzle pieces
that only needed flipping over to make
the picture of the couple in the boat
materialize: early fall, last of summer
sucked down a throat of light, pink,
inner pink, and the man moves his head
down her body and her hands flutter
the water but you're pushing me out,
yanking the door closed, flicking back
your hair as you drive away, weaving over
the center line. I saw that girl
again today, my colleague's student who
looks like you. Same lips shaping Don't,
same eyes daring Enter, same dark luster,
same heavy havoc of hair and each time
I make a fool of myself because I'm thinking
life after death, twenty years about right.
I'm thinking all that time as an attendant
holding my jeweled bowl, now must I turn
to dust? I hate how I must let you go
again, sloshed, stiff-dicked, the night
screaming something indecipherable
on its silver rail, a man across the alley
banging on a door, a dog running by, slipping
from its body and when D comes to find you,

how easy it was to get her into bed, how
functional and quick and her saying, Is that it?
pissed, leaving without her underpants. Blue
as anaesthetic, blue as losing consciousness
and me burrowing back into sleep. I'd barely
remember except for D calling a few hours later,
dawn a mess on the sheets, calling from
the hospital, cursing me, cursing us both.
Something broken and wet wrapped in cotton
inside my head and I'm thinking of those
disinfected floors, the guy going by
with the mop, the pay phone mouthpiece hot
with D's words and the words of the person
she waited behind and the other calls
she'll have to make, your best friend.
I say the first name of your father and
see him riding by on his mower while she raves
and weeps and you're closed in a drawer and
I'm hating myself for already forgiving myself,
for thinking if only you'd stayed, come in,
had let me, let me, let me, juice would be
still dripping down our necks.

The Last I Heard of My Father

Sometimes it's choking him in a dream.
Sometimes it's sprouting wings,
getting high enough to see the dump all at once,
gulls breaking back and forth like waves
in front of the bulldozer. Sometimes
it's pounding nails into the giant heart.
Every night from 2 to 3 a part of me
watches the movie about the head kept alive
in a tray. Lots of tubes moving liquid around.
If Ray Milland isn't in it, he should be.
Whatever happened to Ray Milland? I bet one day
he sat down with his awards and realized
he'd played a lot of drunks and scientists
in circumstances involving heads kept alive
in trays and decided he needed a rest
from the public eye. So this head wants
to be dead but no one will let it, even
the doctor's got these extreme expectations,
you've got these extreme expectations,
I've got these extreme expectations.
We were almost to the point of mutual
respect. We were almost to the point of blows.

All Told

News of her death
comes obscured with radiance
as if delivered by God's messenger.
The heart struggles with depictions,
scarves fly from her mouth
as the car hits the tree at 70.
For hours, content just lies there,
a butterfly smashed in a dictionary.
Phantom cauldrons pour molten leads
through the air. There is a narrowing,
a soaking with fiercer color.
God puts everything on the anvil.
A definition is a sorry thing but
we will all be redefined. Someone
cuts the stems of lilies
for a shallow vase. Someone else
comes home, wet from walking in the fog.

Instructions for Living

You will never know enough.
You will never know when to stop.
One day you'll wake mid-afternoon
distant from yourself as if some
switch has occurred in the nouns
of the summer novel of your life. You've become
a log hauled from the brawling surf,
no, someone named Myrtle, no, a needy
translucent thing squawling
in the yellow tub. You must be patient
even though within you is a launching,
a propulsion like some favorite song
played in a waiting room to drown out
the drill. At some point everything will
be danced to. Violins rush forward
seeming to recognize you. Music and limping,
disruption and joy, it is best to alternate
although there is also sweetness
in saying a name over and over again
when you're alone and miserable in Peru.
Peru, Indiana that is. Do not
be afraid of being ridiculous.
The pharoahs were ridiculous yet
they managed to live almost forever,
their servants stuffed beside them
to assure their every pleasure. But pleasure
is just a way of residing in the temporary
body, changing the water in bright vases,
snipping snapdragon stems. There are two
kinds of people but you may be neither,
athwart with yearning like a broken window,
I mean how the wind comes in ransacking,
not excluding or deciding, the written-

down things crumbling into structures.
Ice would be nice. To each a grinchy
world of piazzas. Rope-skipping
pickpockets. Foam. Today is Friday,
yesterday it rained. Where do you live?
My name is Diego. Half the time
there will be no equivalent
in any language you know.
Do not despair overly.
Let the mouth shape the omnivorous Oh.
It is always raining inside the sea.
Love without reason. Grapes
wither in the fridge, curtains
riffle behind some fleeing,
the never-actually-there banging.
It is always raining inside me.
The children are not children anymore
yet it seems only yesterday we were they
yielding the irrational at our desks,
our bodies producing red berries and thorns,
the operations conveyed by squiggly lines.
There is an aster in disaster which is
the eye of God. Even God gropes along,
blinded each spring, blossoms of rain
forming in front of your nose while
you wait on the platform, all the women
suddenly wearing pink hats. Who
are you there to meet? Yourself, of course,
who is always late, never has an umbrella.
Often you'll feel about to glimpse
what it's all about,
some truth beyond the scrolling of fact:
diamonds made from compressed coal, coal
compressed herbaceous mass eons old.
A great lens fits over the head
like that contraption of the opthalmologist
who asks after each adjustment, Better? Better?
until, alas, you haven't a clue,

what you focused on never became a word
and that sentence that looked about to flood
with meaning just shifts like dust, rift dirt,
the *I am Here* some fool wrote on the side of his boat
to fix where he caught the fish that seemed
the body of a god, that actually spoke,
"Each must sigh for accessible bliss,"
know nothing and conceal." Whatever
that means. All is urging, an augury
we no longer possess the skill or
flimflammery to read. Things just
spill their guts into the galvanized tray
and die, occasionally revealing some marvel
in what they swallowed. Who'd a thunk it?
Khlebnikov got to the point where
he was writing only numbers. Often
as you near the end of what you're saying,
you'll find you're saying something else
to the frowns of those on the ridge
asking which way to the bridge.
The cold bothers you more and more.
You're struggling with a door.
It is the end of summer, the storm
the radio vowed never materializes,
a hammock swings between trees.
One wakes crying from a dream
of her father come back, another hears
not knowing what. One names few stars
and those uncertainly.

Servant's Return

Because I survived the octopus
simmered in lamb's blood, iridescent
roe rolled in dog's tongue, pressed
brine of duck brain gelled over figs
stuffed with purple mushrooms, black
fish, bear testicle, infusions of wine,

my lord was able to eat. And because
my lord survived and advances,
I am permitted this return

but on the first morning, barely beyond
the gates, sparrows in a cherry bower
singing phantom songs, phantom sparrows,
the fruit pecked open, neglected, bleeding,
inebriating the air. On the second day,

quivering heat, a man kneeling in a plot
of thorns glares up at the clink
of my bracelets, face like ice
on a puddle. Eggs broken
on one narrow pass, grotesques

just formed, things with flippers and
horns, eight legs. The few laborers I pass
bent under burdens too great to look up from
yet they carry only bundles of dry grass.
Every beggar silent. A mule lashed

to a broken tree, half skeleton, but
not grazing the flowers at its hooves.
And on the evening of the fifth day,

in the doorway of the home I was
taken from, an old woman pretending
to be my mother, pretending to cry.

Post-Ovidian

The last I remember is drinking
one of those minty things then
watching owls hunch up and feed
each other proving once again

love makes even the wisest
ridiculous. Dusk, the first
bituminous dust rising from
the ashen forms of things.

I believe the things themselves
do not exist but that doesn't mean
I let anyone push me around.
Actually, I remember everything,

the sky drawing its silk-wrapped blade
across its gut spilling red contaminants
into the bay, the moon dumping out
its fullness and who's going to clean

this mess up? Often I feel dwarfed
by my tasks but she thought I said
dwarfed by my tusks and felt she could help,
the young public defender. Not

that I intended to kill anything
when I charged into the lake.
All was music, raw scraping wheel,
the nubby feel of her shirt, hormonal

arias, the honey pours over the lip,
smothering the feasting ant.
One moment you're the honey,
the next you're the ant. Funny thing

about strangling a swan
is under the feathers,
there's nearly no neck at all.
In the middle distance, what looks like

crowbars fleeing larger crowbars.
Beauty is always disasterous
in California in February, houses
reel up the muddy hills on stilts,

the nipple lowers to the mouth and
for the hundredth time, it's your last chance.
You're reinacting a failed astral life.
It doesn't exactly cough but there is

a last occluded breath then all
is silent except the fading elegiac
honking of the other swans, your love
beside you like one wrestled from a cloud.

Exquisite Corpse

Each morning a rose.
Each evening a fluorochlorohydrocarbon.
Some afternoons I'd rather not be
a triangle in a hammock, each side
pressing in upon the other like a family.
The phone rings. Perhaps it would be better
to be the goat, surrounded by electric fence,
prodigiously feeding. The goat fears not
what is unseen. Some impurities make
water clearer. At the center is warm bleeting
just as at the center of the poem is
the person, one ill-adjusted, craven
ball of nerves releasing a great squirt of ink
like a cornered squid. To clean a squid,
pull the head away from the body, cut
the tentacles just below the eyes and reserve
the body sac. A pinkish brown emotes.
The goat gambols in the sourgrass.
The triangle would rather not answer the phone.
At the center is warm bleeting like a memory
of fucking on a rainy afternoon. Illicit,
misty gists. And then my eyes which were already
open would open on scenes of such unspeakable
eroticism I'd come immediately lashingly
not necessarily inside her on top of her
in her mouth sometimes on her back her breasts
her hair the sheets and her coming in response
or already during and then we'd fall
apart afraid of ourselves and not looking
at each other then looking at each other
as if over a cliff the water below thrashing
the hawks stooping the renaissance moveable
type afraid not just of her husband or missing
the last train. The last two weeks of May

then my aunt died and I had to go back to
Kalamazoo. I remember us eating only once,
crunchy, early strawberries and one night
it snowed. Certainly the ropes
hanging from the clouds indicative
of some further tolling. But when I got back,
she seemed like something in a gallery. You either
look at the blue watery shape and weep or
don't put a dollar in the lucite box by the door.
It's not a matter of convincing anyone.
My aunt actually thought God was white.
In her apartment, I poured her perfumes
down the drain, threw the swan-shaped,
diamond-shaped, flame-shaped bottles
into the recycling. Subatomicly, it's all
collision upon collision, explosion and
reconstitution until a dead thing becomes
a harpsichord. You can tell a principle's
at work by the pyramidal shape of olives
crammed in a jar, the 120-degree angles
at which things shatter, the oils pooling
like wrung-out rainbows. Sometimes, it's best
to just get out of the way. The kind of day
you need both sunglasses and umbrella
but have neither have neither have neither.
A blue scum forms on the horizon and
in your hand is a number for the butcher.
I went to see the doctor. There's a hole in my heart.

First You Must

Before the abstract cone enfiladed
in blue enthusiasms, you must learn
to draw a tree that looks like a tree.
But first you must study bark
at the Institute of Bark in Amsterdam.
You must learn the woody organelles in Dutch
although first you must be immunized.
Luckily this is not the 14th century
and you are trying to become a doctor of the throat
as you would have only the bodies of hanged thieves
to cut apart and hanging makes a mess
of the mechanisms of the throat. Hope
may be depicted as a cinder block wrapped
in aluminum foil which is pretty
rotten luggage. First you'll
fall in love with what you can't
understand. The baby ram butts the shiny tractor.
Nothing you draw looks like anything else.
First you must build a cathedral of toothpicks.
Write nothing but sonnets for a year.
The error is not to fall but to fall
from an ungreat height. First you must fall
for the girl like you on the boat
seeming to leave all she knows but also
unlike you in some important, not only
glandular, ways. The days grow short, icier,
the heart like a ram in a field surrounded by electric
wire. The single tree there in the wind
not looking much like a tree, full
of withered fruit vexed with caterpillars.
It resembles a tragic wig.
No verse is actually free.
Before oils, charcoal. First you must go

to Vermeer's birthplace. Bed linens crusty,
widows a-wink with all you do not know
like a horrible disease lurking in the genes.
I must know, you shout, shaking the girl hard.
This is a mistake. What she first thought
was your handsome intensity, she now thinks
is insanity. First you must be forgiven.
Before being a human being, you must be
a zygote. Ditto a horse, a ram, an alligator.
The tractor comes into the world from a pit of fire
like the trombone. Better than you have failed.
The girl hurries off in a form of native dress
you know not the word for. The test returns
with a big red X. Before watching the sun set
into the ocean of tears, you must study
optics. Sir Isaac Newton knew a lot about optics
before he knew a lot about gravity and orbits.
What will make the girl return? And you call
yourself an artist. First you must suffer,
first the form in duplicate. Before the form,
the pre-form. Before crying forlorn forlorn,
rigor mortis. Before tackling the nude,
you must work for months with wooden blocks.

Clangor

I won't believe the frog brought forth
by the morning mist or any other proclamation
of spring, pink frowsy eucalyptus blooms,
leaves clattering in the breeze like
dropped swords. No, I won't surrender
or resist, prowling through the shouted
slogans of the avenues, the collapsed
holding forth their wounds like advertisements
for wounds, advertisements for help
I cannot give. I will not give.
Rachitic, bleary, sobbed-out,
I'm a cloud of doubt, no rain inside
to feather the hills with green,
florescent lichen climbing the singed trees
on the ridge where the fire quit. I won't
believe any fire or light, particle or wave,
no universe of string, body of water, cure.
Not the recurring dream of my father
trying to reach me through the burning door
or what he would say if he could, what
counsel of dirt, how naive it is to think
we die just once. I'll believe nothing
that comes from any mouth, not mine,
not yours. Even the context won't tell
the difference between tear and tear.
In the apartment below, the student
of divinity plays his chants. You think
I know what to do? Mock oranges
saturate the wrung air. You think
I could live without you?

Against Classicism

I don't want to remember her
often because each remembering
seems an erosion, a kind of erasing:

a shoe is lost, a voice; an arm drags
across the drawing drawing, a word
repeated leaks sense. The first week

after, I said her name a hundred times.
Wasn't there once a boat in the smudgy
surge? And a hand, wasn't there a hand?

Thus the hole that might have been a mouth
fills with seed that sprouts obdurant
thistle, insinuations of cracks; thus

a bit of mirror fixed into what
might have been the socket of an eye.
It is always raining when I remember,

raining on a beach, sand pocked and worn
further by waves going over going over
and more and more who I call to, who

I ask seems a fabrication of putty.
Gray gulls the color of this weather.

I Know My Friends Will Laugh

but I think there's so much spirit-stuff in this world that even
the dust kicked up on the trail above Tomales swirls and
maneuvers and gestures, alive for an instant because to be
alive is always for an instant.

My friends will say I've been in California too long but within
the dust there's some further puffing up as the love in any
of us puffs up for the ineffable because love is always for
the ineffable even when she's giggling in your arms, your
tongue in her ear.

Not the likelihood of not loving enough—stone dark with
condensed fog—although that too is spirit's residing,
another lease, detective novels abandoned on the shelf,
pages falling out, binding crust, silverfish flashing.

Because when the spirit is divided, torn apart as it seems it
must be, the head keeps singing in the lion's mouth even as
the body, fallen to its knees, pats the ground for some
dropped key, some broken jewelry, each tooth and claw
mark a new mouth, new eyelids opening on the next world.

I'm not even sure there is a next world.

Perhaps death is just unloosening, release, the way the rose
petals all drop at once just as Christina said they would.

Part of me says nothing like these petals and dust, part of me
says everything petals and dust.

By now my friends are nearly choking on their beers but part of
me sees my father's chawed face the day they brought him
home from the golf course like something God bit, didn't
like, threw back.

Part of me sees supper laid out while I shake snow from my coat.

Sees dusk ignite cattails into sheaves of light.

Sees the ant's entrance through the smashed owl's eye into
    Byzantium.

My friends, what should I believe? Even the lice are trembling.

Frottage

How goofy and horrible is life. Just
look into the faces of the lovers
as they near their drastic destinations,
the horses lathered and fagged. Just
look at them handling the vase
priced beyond the rational beneath
the sign stating the store's breakage
policy, and what is the rational but
a thing we must always break? I am not
the only one composed of fractious murmurs.
From the point of view of the clouds,
it is all inevitable and dispersed—
they vanish over the lands to reconstitute
over the seas, themselves again
but no longer themselves, what they wanted
they no longer want, daylight fidgets
across the frothy waves. Most days
you can't even rub a piece of charcoal
across paper laid on some rough wood
without a lion appearing, a fish's umbrella
skeleton. Once we believed it told us
something of ourselves. Once we even believed
in the diagnostic powers of ants. Upon
the eyelids of the touched and suffering,
they'd exchange their secretive packets
like notes folded smaller than chemicals
the dancers pass while dancing with another.
A quadrille. They told us nearly nothing
which may have been enough now that we know
so much more. From the point of view
of the ant, the entire planet is a dream
quivering beneath an eyelid and who's to say
the planet isn't. From the point of view
of the sufferer, it seems everything will

be taken from us except the sensation
of being crawled over. I believe everything
will be taken from us. Then given back
when it's no longer what we want. We
are clouds, and terrible things happen
in clouds. The wolf's mouth is full
of strawberries, the morning's a phantom
hum of glories.

White Crane

I don't need to know any more about death
from the Japanese beetles
infesting the roses and plum
no matter what my neighbor sprays
in orange rubber gloves.
You can almost watch them writhe and wither,
pale and fall like party napkins
blown from a table just as light fades,
and the friends,
as often happens when light fades,
talk of something painful, glacial, pericardial,
and the napkins blow into the long grass.
When Basho writes of the long grass,
I don't need to know it has to do with death,
the characters reddish-brown and dim,
shadows of a rusted sword, an hour hand.
Imagine crossing mountains in summer snow
like Basho, all you own
on your back: brushes, robe,
the small gifts given in parting it's bad luck to leave behind.
I don't want to know what it's like to die on a rose,
sunk in perfume and fumes,
clutching,
to die in summer with everything off its knees,
daisies scattered like eyesight by the fence,
gladiolas open and fallen in mud,
weighed down with opening and breeze.
I wonder what your thoughts were, Father,
after they took your glasses and teeth,
all of us bunched around you like clouds
knocked loose of their moorings,
the white bird lying over you,
its beak down your throat.
Rain, heartbeats of rain.

One Story

In one story, the coyote sings us into being.
The self is either a single arrow shot
into the sun or a long, squiggly thing
wet at one end. If someone were
to rip the roof off and look down on us,
we'd look like lice on a tribal mask.
Now Lorca, there was a poet. The disordered
strength of the curved water, he wrote
shortly before he was shot in the head.
Maybe distorted. We know he held hands
with a school teacher, also shot, and how
the last hour he was sure he'd be shot
and sure he'd be released. At the last moment,
Van Gogh slashed crows across the wheat field.
Winter is scary enough but to follow it with Spring . . .
God must be demented, he must spend a lot of time
out in the cosmic downpour. I mean what
would you do if you had to create Beauty?
I'm afraid I'd start screaming, the most irksome
forms of insects coming from my mouth. I'm afraid
I'd come up with Death. On my desk
is a paper weight, a copse of glass flowers inside.
The last few months my father amassed a collection
of paperweights. He knew he was going to disappear.
Finally my mother said, Take a couple.
I don't think I have the proper papers to weight.
The other is a pewter frog.
It was May, I was 19, writing
a paper on Hamlet for a professor who'd hang himself.
I remember the funeral director asking
my sister and me if we wanted to see my father
one last time. I thought for a moment
it was a serious offer. But he was talking about
a corpse. A corpse in make-up. But this year,

I will get it right, I will stare at a single branch
for all of May. I will know what it's going through
at least on the fructifying surface. In May
he bought a yellow suit he wore just once.
In May I will listen to the bark whimper and split,
the blossoms blink from sleep. I will
haunt the town I've haunted for years,
turning the corner of Sixth and
Grant, seeing myself just ahead
in that ratty jean jacket, sleeve ripped
to fit over the cast. A few pains remain,
become formalized, enacted in dance
but I'm careful not to catch myself. He might
want to get me high in the middle of the day.
I might have work to do, I might be going to the ash
I planted over my dead cat years back
behind the garden where Nancy lost the ring
my father made from a quarter during the war.
She will be sobbing, digging among the infant tomatoes.
It's okay, I will say and she will nod and vanish.
It's all right, I will say and my cat will cease
mewing beneath the earth.